Amazing Job Interview

Job Interview lessons from the Bible

I invite you in a fascinating journey throughout the Bible to
discover how many men and women made the most of the
opportunity that was presented to them to be catapulted into
their destiny. It's all about divine appointments and the
opportunity to show that you are the right person for the right
environment, at the right time. After all, this is the main
purpose of a job interview.

Content

Introduction - Surviving job loss

At the time when this book is written, unemployment is growing rapidly in most parts of the world, bringing its potential damage effects that could range from anxiety to depression and debts; to name just a few.

As a consequence, many people face job interviews in an unfavorable mental state, which doesn't help them to secure a new job.

Does the Bible contain any keys to surviving job loss?

Can the Bible be of any help at all for this situation?

The answer is a resounding YES!

There is a powerful principle taught by Jesus, which should be a great source of encouragement and hope for all the unemployed people.

But even more importantly, it teaches practical steps that can be followed by anyone, whether they are on the verge of losing their jobs or after the job loss.

The parable relates the story of a man (a manager of resources) who was about to lose his job for lack of competency and diligence. We all know the terrible effects of unemployment.

Luke 16:1-3 He also said to His disciples: "There was a certain rich man who had a steward, and an accusation was brought to him that this man was wasting his goods.

So he called him and said to him, 'What is this I hear about you? Give an account of your stewardship, for you can no longer be steward.'

"Then the steward said within himself, 'What shall I do? For my master is taking the stewardship away from me. I cannot dig; I am ashamed to beg.

Upon hearing the bad news, the man begins to analyze the remaining possibilities for him to earn a living and doesn't find any satisfactory one. He is not confident about getting a new job due to lack of proper skills and he can't become a beggar either.

His prospects of surviving job loss didn't look good, on the surface.

Most of you, even if you are unemployed now, don't have it as bad as the steward. You probably have enough skills to get hired again.

But let's examine the rest of the story. It is simply amazing.

Luke 16:4-9 'I have resolved what to do, that when I am put out of the stewardship, they may receive me into their houses.'

"So he called every one of his master's debtors to him, and said to the first, 'How much do you owe my master?'

And he said, 'A hundred measures of oil.' So he said to him, 'Take your bill, and sit down quickly and write fifty.'

Then he said to another, 'And how much do you owe?' So he said, 'A hundred measures of wheat.'

And he said to him, 'Take your bill, and write eighty.'

So the master commended the unjust steward because he had dealt shrewdly. For the sons of this world are more shrewd in their generation than the sons of light.

"And I say to you, make friends for yourselves by unrighteous mammon, that when you fail, they may receive you into an everlasting home.

In his state of despair and anxiety towards his future, the man made an assessment of all the valuable things that could favor him and found two good ones: the outstanding amount owned by his boss's debtors and the relationship he has developed with them over time.

Then, he didn't lose any time. He quickly made individual appointments with the debtors in order to invest in each one of them a rebate on the remaining debt owned.

What we can highlight also from the story is that the level of the rebate was different from one debtor to the other: some got a 50% rebate on the remaining debt, while others only got 20% rebate.

I believe this detail is there to show us that the rebate was not sowed (granted) randomly, but on purpose, according to his knowledge about the capacity of each one.

This is a systematic and wise application of a powerful spiritual principle that I have discovered from the Bible and have named <u>the principle of Ruth's heart</u>.

I have covered this principle more in details in a book, scheduled to be released very soon, in the next few weeks. It is entitled "Overcoming despair".

Five steps to surviving job loss

Surviving job loss through the application of the principle of Ruth's heart requires the following five steps:

• As a first step, the man made a self-assessment of all the valuable things he could give (sow) in somebody else.

• As a second step, if the self-assessment brings many things you can invest, you need to evaluate the potential of each and select only a few. In the case of the steward, he selected a rebate of the outstanding debt balance

• As a third step, he made a brainstorm to find out the ideal profile of the groups of people he can invest into. In his case, it was his boss's debtors

• As a fourth step, he determined an implementation strategy for his investment (same amount to everyone or personalized amount?).

• As a fifth step, he quickly took action.

What is also amazing in the story is that the boss wasn't mad at his steward taking upon himself the authority to give rebates on his boss's money.

Rather, the boss praised the wisdom of his employee, in choosing to apply the principle of Ruth's heart as a solution to overcoming job loss.

And in His conclusion about this parable, Jesus also praised the steward through this statement: ***"And I say to you, make friends for yourselves by unrighteous mammon, that when you fail, they may receive you into an everlasting home» (Luke 16:9)***

We can extract a powerful sub-principle from that statement alone:

Even if you are currently employed, it would be very beneficial to you to perform the skills self-assessment exercise and start investing your skills in other people.

You can do that, while still employed.

The best way to coping with job loss is to be fully prepared before it comes, if it does. There is no such thing as job security anymore.

Skills self-assessment

Skills self-assessment is one the most important steps you can take in order to have good success in your job interviews.

Psalms 126:5-6 (NKJV)Those who sow in tears shall reap in joy.

He who continually goes forth weeping, Bearing seed for sowing, Shall doubtless come again with rejoicing, bringing his sheaves with him

Usually, our times of unemployment are not time of great rejoicing. They are rather times filled with anxieties about our future. For some people, they are even times of despair.

In the verses above, a picture is painted of someone who is in distress (tears) but who is determined to sow seed anyway, despite his unfavorable conditions.

The verses carry a powerful promise of turnaround in the circumstances of the person. **The end condition of the person is very positive, he gets the results (harvest) of his action (sowing) and he is filled with joy**.

I hope you are greatly encouraged by these verses. This is a psalm for job interview.

"But wait a minute, Does sowing seed in tears have anything to do with job interview?" I can imagine the question in the mind of many.

Let's extract together the amazing treasures contained in these verses. By the time we finish, you will see the connection.

A seed is something valuable, that you decide to put in the ground, in the hope that it will produce results for you. The results are much greater than the seed itself.

If you are currently unemployed, and in distress about your condition, then you are the sower in tears.

Now the next question is: what is the seed?

Before answering the question, let me insure you that you have a seed. Actually, you have many seeds.

What I mean is that you have many valuable things inside of you that are potential seeds that can be sowed.

To discover these seeds, you have to follow the skills self-assessment processes.

If you follow the powerful principle taught in these verses, you will see a complete turnaround in your situation.

You will see a positive outcome and will rejoice.

Skills self-assessment processes

All the skills and competencies self-assessment processes are organized around the following questions you need to ask yourself :

- What are my strengths?

- What are the skills I have developed during my career or in other circumstances?

- What good qualities people usually praise me for?

- What are the things I do better than most people?

- What are the things I know I have inside of me, even if they have not been demonstrated yet?

It is critical that you document your answers and for each skill, put in writing as many details as possible about the circumstances where you demonstrated those skills.

To help you in that exercise, you can use one of the many self-assessment techniques named CARD.

The first step of the CARD technique is to make a list of all of your accomplishments (whether in a professional setting or in your personal life).

What are you proud of?

The second step is to start analyzing these accomplishments in order to extract the following elements (the Context, the Actions taken, the Results, the Demonstrated skills)

C stands for the Context of the accomplishment. What was the situation? What was the problem?

A stands for the actions you took in the situation

R stands for the results of your action

D stands for Demonstration. Which skills and competencies are demonstrated through this?

At the end, you get what you were exactly looking for: a documented list of your skills and competencies that can help you write a good CV and perform well during job interviews. For example, this list will help you tremendously to provide a great and argumented answer to the following job interview questions:

- What are your strengths?

- Tell me about 3 accomplishments that you are the most proud of and why

What is The perfect job interview for you?

First, let's examine the purpose of job interviews anyway. **The main purpose is to validate a perfect fit between a candidate and a prospective employer.** It is also a way for each of the two parties involved to get to know each other better. With that in mind, how would you describe the ideal job interview for you? Let's go back in history, to examine the first that ever happened in human history.

Genesis 1:28 God blessed them and said to them, "Be fruitful and increase in number; fill the earth and subdue it. Rule over the fish of the sea and the birds of the air and over every living creature that moves on the ground."

Would you say that Adam had a perfect job interview? He was never asked about his qualifications and past experiences. Luckily enough because he did not have any past experiences. The CEO of the universe just handed over to him the job description (**Genesis 1:28**), the compensation and benefits package and offered him the job. The CEO of the universe declared him capable to perform well on the job; Adam was the right man, no doubt about it.

What made the difference? How it that Adam was never is questioned about his qualifications and past experiences related to the job? Simply because the CEO knew him well enough to declare him fit for the position.

Wouldn't it be nice to walk in the job interview knowing you were fit for the position and even more importantly, knowing your interviewer was also aware of this fact?

But usually, it doesn't happen this way. We need to get to know the interviewer and the company better and vice versa. The perfect job interview for me is the one which serves this main purpose. It may not always turn out like it did with Adam. You may realize you did not want to work for this employer. It is best to find this out sooner than later. It is best to find it out during the interview rather that after you have taken the position.

After all, you need also to know the company's perspective for the future. If there is a high turnover for the position you are applying for, there may be an issue, either with the management or the responsibilities assigned for the position itself. Adam did not have this issue. He was offered a brand new position that has just been created by the CEO. This position was made necessary by the expansion the company was going through. So, the perspectives for the future of the employer were great.

You also need to find out the potential for growth and personal development. What about an exponential potential of growth (multiplication) like the CEO described to Adam? Yes, I know it doesn't happen often. You might still be satisfied with incremental growth (addition).

Finally, you need to know to whom you will be reporting to, and also how much responsibility you will have (how many people will be reporting to you). Adam had all this information during his interview. He knew he was to rule a huge division of the company. Wow! Talk about a perfect job interview! He got to see his future offices (the Garden of Eden) and all the multiple streams of income flowing to it (the 4 rivers described in **Genesis 2:10-14**).

He got immediate hands-on training on how to rule the division when the CEO brought him all the products offerings and ask him to label them and give them a name (**Genesis 2:19-20**). He was to keep all the profits from the division expect a small percentage. Wow! Talk about huge stock options. Adam was proposed an offer he couldn't refuse!!!

What are the key lessons to learn from the first job interview that ever happened?
• There is still hope for you if you don't have any past experiences
• You can get a job offer you can't refuse
• You can get hands-on training right from the beginning
• You can get to work for the perfect employer

But you still need to get prepared for the worst:
• Think about any good questions to ask to know if there is a good fit with the company, if you would like and flourish on the job, if the company would last for long
• And, be prepared to demonstrate why you are the best candidate for the position, explain your past experiences in details and how they are relevant.

In the next pages, using the book of books, i.e. the Bible, we will get into deep details about all the different aspects of the job interview and how to be successful in it, knowing when to speak and when to listen, when to answer unasked questions and when not to provoke loads of questions you can't answer (our friend Job from the book of Job will help us on that one:-:-)), how to detect positive or negative signals, how to use your body language to your best advantage, how to give a positive first impression, how to succeed in the tests you may have to go through during the job interview.

In a nutshell, I will lead you through a fascinating journey of discovery on how the Bible is the best resource for successful job interview and what we can learn from the great characters that are portrayed in it. You will also come to realize that all employers in the

Bible don't measure up to the CEO of the universe; you will meet the good, the bad and the ugly with always a practical learning as a takeaway. Let's start this fascinating journey together, on the way to the perfect job interview!

Job Interview Tips

What are the top 10 job interview tips?

Job Interview Tip 1: Success is 80% preparation - Be prepared

This first and most important tip may surprise you because it starts way before the interview and has several aspects to it.

In effect, a big part in succeeding in your interview is achieved before the interview itself. A good preparation will be key to your success. All the details count; starting for the clothing you will wear which should be appropriate for the job, to your attitude, the visualization of your success. To demonstrate your interest in the company, you should conduct some research (via the internet) and questions you will ask. You should also know how to answer the most common questions, magnifying your strengths and minimizing the relevance of your weaknesses in succeeding in the job.

Job Interview Tip 2: First (minute) impression is everything

The second element of the top 10 job interview tips may seem obvious but is critical. Managers generally have a job candidate sized up within minutes of the start of an interview, according to survey results.

- You will only get one opportunity to make a positive first impression, take advantage of it. The following elements are key to achieve this: smile, firm handshake, enthusiasm, confidence, look the other person in the eyes, dress appropriately (we will come back later with top tips to dress appropriately for job interview)

- Greet the secretary and be courteous (she may have to give her opinion about the different candidates).

Job Interview Tip 3: Establish a good rapport with the interviewer

- The third piece of the job interview tips should not surprise you: **People hire people they can get along with.**

This includes knowing when to speak and when to keep quiet. The interviewer is trying to see if you are fit for the job and also fit for the company. He/she may be your next boss, and also want to know if he/she can get along with you

- Watch the body language and signs (either good or bad) and adjust accordingly. You may need to elaborate more on some answers and be briefer on others. This is particularly true when answering open questions such as: tell me more about yourself.

- **What you do speaks so loudly what you say I can't hear!**. This is especially true during a job interview. Use your behavior to your advantage during the interview. Judges 7:5 relates the story of Gideon, when God teaches him how to select the 300 men for the battle. these guys didn't know the way they drank water was actually part of the selection process. It showed something about them that was a critical skill for the job. This is called behavioral job interview that we will cover in another section of the site. (In consequence, be alert to your own body language and also the one of the interviewer because it is revealing things about you)

- Don't argue with the interviewer. Don't engage in expert debates. We will look more into how to go around such difficult times and how not to argue even though you know the other person is wrong. The key is to identify which part this will play in the evaluation of your candidature.

- Keep your emotions under control, even when asked

illegal questions. We will be covering specifically this topic later.

- Be honest but positive in answering tough questions such as: what are your defaults? There may be some weak areas in your candidature; you may not have enough experience, enough education. You will need to convince the interviewer that you can make up for these weak areas. Give example on how you succeeded in the past in similar situations but don't deny the existence of these weak areas.

Job Interview Tip 4: Ask the good questions
- The fourth of the top 10 job interview tips will demonstrate your preparation and interest in the company. This is when you will make the best use of all the information you gathered about the company before the job interview.
- Enquire about the resources that will be available to you if you get hired to succeed in the job.
- Ask for clarifications on the job description. (cf Moses: if the Israelites ask me who sent me, what should I answer them?)

Job Interview Tip 5: Use wisdom to answer unasked questions
- Most job interview tips overlook this critical one which can make all the difference between a good and a great job interview. Your interviewer may be lacking experience or may just have forgotten. If you feel some strong areas in favor of your candidature have not been addressed, feel free to bring it up. Usually, you'll get the opportunity when the person asks you if you have something else to ask. You will be helping the person make a more qualified decision and he/she will be graceful to you for it.

Job Interview Tip 6: Make a summary at the end restating why you are the best candidate

- Not the least of the job interview tips, this piece gives you the opportunity to close with style.

A good interviewer will give you the opportunity at the end to summarize your strengths in relation to the job. So, be prepared for it. This is also the opportunity to demonstrate your active listening skills, to show your attention to the key points the interviewer thinks are necessary to succeed in the job.

Job Interview Tip 7: Ask about the next steps on the hiring process

- The seventh job interview tip is not critical but should not be ignored. You need to know when you can expect a decision, if there would be some more interviews to come

Job Interview Tip 8: Send a thank you letter as a follow up (no later than 1 day after the interview)

- This is also a golden opportunity to answer some unasked questions and restate your interest in the position and why you are the best candidate

Job Interview Tip 9: Use open questions to your advantage

– Questions such as "Tell me more about yourself", "Tell me about your past experiences". Salesmen know it very well, don't describe features but benefits. You are the product during the job interview. One of the top tips is to always relate what you are saying to how it will benefit the company. Don't ever assume anything. Make it easy for your interviewer to identify the best fit areas.

– "Do you have anything else to add?" is an open invitation to summarize your strengths in relation to the job. Don't miss it.

Job Interview Tip 10: Get ready for the next steps

- The last element of the top 10 job interview tips may seem obvious, but the interview was not an end in itself. It may lead to another one with a different emphasis. Be ready to take some tests. It could happen also that the interviewer calls you back to clarify certain points. This is all good signs, so be prepared for it. You may also need to advise some of your referrals that they may get a call for the interviewer.
- Be ready also to suggest a salary range if you get asked. On this point, the opinions diverge if this point should be brought up during the job interview itself.

In conclusion: Even though not an exact science, the top 10 job interview tips described above should get you closer to your goal. Depending on the situation, some of the tips may not apply.

A compelling thank you letter

One thing many candidates forget is to send a job interview thank you letter. Let's learn from a short story, how one man distinguished himself from 9 others by the simple fact of giving thanks.

Luc 17:12 Then as He entered a certain village, there met Him ten men who were lepers, who stood afar off.

Luc 17:13 **And they lifted up** *their* **voices and said, "Jesus, Master, have mercy on us!"**

Luc 17:14 **So when He saw** *them,* **He said to them,** "Go, show yourselves to the priests." **And so it was that as they went, they were cleansed.**

Luc 17:15 **And one of them, when he saw that he was healed, returned, and with a loud voice glorified God,**

Luc 17:16 **and fell down on** *his* **face at His feet, giving Him thanks. And he was a Samaritan.**

Luc 17:17 **So Jesus answered and said,** "Were there not ten cleansed? But where *are* the nine?

Luc 17:18 Were there not any found who returned to give glory to God except this foreigner?"

Luc 17:19 **And He said to him,** "Arise, go your way. Your faith has made you well."

10 of them were qualified to receive their healing (they had faith for healing), only one was qualified to get saved (the one that came back to give thanks).

Similarly, maybe 10 of you will be qualified to get an interview but if you are the only one sending a thank you letter, you might as well be the only one qualified to get hired.

But beyond showing your gratitude to the interviewer, the letter is also a golden opportunity to position yourself ahead of the other candidates.

It is an ideal complement to the interview and can help you re-summarize your strengths in regards to the position, provide better answers to some concerns in the mind of the interviewer and demonstrate again your interest for the company and the job.

It also shows your proactiveness.

As you can see, there are many benefits in sending a thank you letter.

With regards to timing, you should send it no later than 24 to 48 hours after the interview. Whenever possible, It should reach the company before they evaluate you after the interview.

The prerequisite for sending the letter is a self-evaluation of your performance during the interview. This should be done right after, while everything is still fresh.

Evaluating your performance

Job interview follow up is as equally as important that proper preparation.

One of the key things we can learn from the Bible is that God always evaluate everything He does, to see if it is according to the plan.

In the book of Genesis, after each day of creation, God took a step back and evaluated what He had just made. And He rated every day as good, except the sixth day which He rated as VERY GOOD. Incidently, that was the day He created man, who was designed to manage His creation for Him.

In the following verses, we can see Jesus doing the same thing while healing a blind man.

Mar 8:22 Then He came to Bethsaida; and they brought a blind man to Him, and begged Him to touch him.
Mar 8:23 So He took the blind man by the hand and led him out of the town. And when He had spit on his eyes and put His hands on him, He asked him if he saw anything.
Mar 8:24 And he looked up and said, "I see men like trees, walking."
Mar 8:25 Then He put *His* hands on his eyes again and made him look up. And he was restored and saw everyone clearly.

He didn't assume anything. He made his evaluation by asking the blind man if he did see anything. Then, He took some corrective actions.

Similarly, after the job interview, it is critical that you evaluate your performance.

Did you have good rapport with the interviewer?

Did you demonstrate good knowledge about the company and a good understanding of what is required by the position?

Did you show your motivation to get the job?

Did you get to know more about the corporate culture?

From the interview, what are the possible concerns in the hiring manager's mind about your candidature? (If the interviewer insists on some particular topics, that should give you a hint. Or maybe, he or she will say something like "on reading your resume, I had some questions about…")

Did you forget to ask some key questions? (For example, you shouldn't leave the interview without a clear idea about the hiring process: what would be the next steps? Will there be any subsequent interviews? How many of them? When should you expect feedback from the company?)

After the fact, do you think of additional strengths you possess that could give you a competitive advantage over the other candidates?

A good job interview follow up will help you write a compelling thank you letter where you can correct whatever was not optimal during the interview.

Successful Job Interview

Let's look from the book of Psalms for 5 keys to a successful job interview

Psalms 1-3 1 Blessed is the man who does not walk in the counsel of the wicked or stand in the way of sinners or sit in the seat of mockers. 2 But his delight is in the law of the LORD, and on his law he meditates day and night.

3 He is like a tree planted by streams of water, which yields its fruit in season and whose leaf does not wither. Whatever he does prospers.

These successful job interview keys can be split in two parts: the external ones and the internal ones.

Successful job interview key 1: Get your thinking right!.

Don't walk in the counsel of the wicked: don't associate with people that don't have their thinking right about job interviews, about companies. The people you associate with will impact the way you think and every success starts from the thinking. If you don't have the right thoughts about the job interview process, you may view it as a confrontation. You will display a defensive attitude, it will be very difficult for you to get a connection with the interviewer.

Successful job interview key 2: Get your acts together!

"Don't stand in the way of sinners" speaks of what you do before, during and after the job interview. Before, you need to be prepared. During, you need to connect with the interviewer, clarify the job position, demonstrate the adequacy of your competencies with the position. You need to have the proper body language to support what you say. After, you need to restate your interest, send a thank you letter and be clear about the next steps.

Successful job interview key 3:Communicate effectively!

Don't sit in the seat of mockers speaks about what you say during the job interview and even more importantly how you say it. Connecting with the interviewer is key and you won't achieve that goal if you display a mocker attitude.

Successful job interview key 4:Show you motivation!

You have to delight in the law of the Lord, you have to show the interviewer your motivation to handle the challenges of the job position. It shouldn't appear that you simply need a job to pay your bills and make a living. The job should not be a law, something you have to do but rather something you like and want to do. In summary, display the right attitude, a positive one.

Successful job interview key 5:Visualize your success!

You need to visualize yourself successful during the job interview and also successfully handling the challenges of the job. This process has to start before the interview and continue afterwards.

Preparing for a job interview

How can one be best preparing for a job interview?

Success is 80% preparation - Be prepared
- Attitude is everything. Come with a positive attitude. It is very positive that you have been invited for a job interview. The company obviously thinks you can be a good fit. Don't show up all defeated. Leave all your doubts at home.

Moses is the perfect example of what not to do when preparing for a job interview. He did not think he was apt for the job. He still had in mind his previous failure when he tried to prove himself as the deliverer of Israel and was rejected. He had to run for his life. He never overcame this failure.

- Then what is the big lesson to learn from Moses experience? Simply stated: One of the greatest ways of preparing for a job interview is a job interview. It sounds strange but it is not. Use past interviews as a preparation. This is why it is critical to post-evaluate each interview: what was good and what you should improve for the future. Don't be discouraged by past failures but instead build up on them.

- You may say: that is all well, but how do I implement above advice?

One of the way is to visualize success during the job interview. You should see yourself displaying the right attitude, giving positive first impression, answering questions with calm and confidence, showing to the interviewer why you are the best fit candidate for the job.
You should see yourself getting the desired result at the end, be it the next interview or been offered the job. David visualized his success in the job and this assurance showed when his answered the objections of Saul the interviewer. - David, in his interview with King Saul, was obviously prepared to answer the most difficult questions he would face: what makes you

think you can do the job? Why should we choose you? Be prepared and review the most difficult questions and the answers you will provide.

- If possible, preparing for a job interview can involve a rehearsal. Do it with somebody you trust that can give you honest feedback.

- Know your weaknesses and be prepared to show the company why they don't disqualify you for the job. Again, David knew he was only a boy, apparently less strongly than giant Goliath, but he showed from his resume, how he overcame in the past this apparent weakness.
In contrary, Moses magnified his weaknesses and failed to recognize his strengths in relation to the job.

- Know very well your resume and how to comment on it and highlight quickly the parts that best qualify you for the job. This is even more critical if, like David, you didn't have the opportunity to submit your resume before the job interview.

- Prepare the appropriate clothes you will wear. Whenever in doubt, be conservative, suit and ties for men. For women, it is critical not to dress in a provocative way.

- Make some research on the company before you come to the interview: what are their most common problems and how can you contribute to solve it? What is the corporate culture? Be ready to show you share the company values. We have a great illustration with David. He showed to Saul his greatest motive for wanting the job is to fight for the honor of the God of Israel. He was saying in effect to the interviewer: not only I know your corporate values and mission, but I totally share them. I can recognize the problem you are facing is a great threat to them (and the very existence of your company) and this will be my motivation to succeed. In a nutshell, he was prepared to answer the HOW (skills) question and the WHY (motivation). He could not be denied!

- Preparing for a job interview also involves taking care of the small details that make all the difference. Be prepared to arrive in time. Make sure you know exactly how to reach the location and if possible, go there the day before and take note of the time it takes.

- Make all the necessary arrangements to arrive early, no later than 15 minutes before the scheduled time.

- Try to know in advance who will be conducting the interview: Will it be your future boss? Will it be HR? Will it be a peer? Will it be an internal client?

- Try to know if it will be a group interview (several interviewers and/or candidates at the same time) or an individual one. Although not always possible, this part of knowing which type of interviewed you will have can be key in terms of preparation. Will you have to go through some tests (behavioral, personality, technical)?

- If relevant, bring with you some tools. David brought his slings and stones to the interview. What are your slings and stones? If you are a paint, you could have to show your work. If you are a web designer, you should be ready to provide the URL of some of your websites. Use to your advantage the following maxim: better be prepared for an opportunity and not have one, than to have an opportunity and not being prepared.

Job Interview Preparation - Be ready to invade Canaan

Amazing keys to successful job interview preparation can be found in the book of Numbers, chapter 13. Let's get the context of the story:

After been delivered from Egypt (place of frustration and dissatisfaction), the children of Israel crossed the Red sea and were preparing to invade the land of Canaan.

But before going into the battle, the leader Moses sent 12 spies into the land with a list of 7 questions.

"Then Moses sent them to spy out the land of Canaan, and said to them, 'Go up this way into the South, and go up to the mountains, and see the land, (1) what it is? (2) Whether the people who dwell in it are strong or weak? (3) Few or many? (4) Whether the land they dwell in is good or bad? (5) Whether the cities they inhabit are tents or strongholds? (6) Whether the land is fat or lean? (7) And whether there is any wood? Be of good courage and bring some of the fruit of the land.'" **Numbers 13:17-20**

Let's uncover from this passage some keys to successful job interview preparation through preliminary research on the company.

1. **What it is** (the land of Canaan represents your prospective employer)

You need to know everything possible about your prospective employer. What are their most common problems? What is their position within their industry? What is their image? Nowadays most companies have a corporate website. This is a great place to start your research.

You need also to find as much information as possible on the position. This part of the job interview preparation is expected of you. It shows your interest in the company and the position.

2. **Whether the people who dwell in it are strong or weak? Few or many?**

(the people who dwell in the land represents your competition). It could be the other candidates for the job. It could be the person who occupied previously the position. It could simply be the mindset of your interviewer. What are the obstacles between you and the position. You need to know what they are and their amplitude. Are they big obstacles or small ones? How many are they (few or many ?) What are their strengths and weaknesses? You can ask the following questions to the interviewer: What did you like most about the person who occupied this position before? What did you like less about him?

3. **Whether the land they dwell in is good or bad?**
This is an overall evaluation of the position. Don't forget any element. Is this an employer you will be happy to work for? What are the perspectives for career evolution ? What is the morale of their current employees? Obviously, to get this part of job interview preparation right, you may need to contact one of their employees. This is not always possible.

4. **Whether the cities they inhabit are tents or strongholds?**
How big are the feet of the person whose shoes you are stepping into? Which marks have they left on the position? Which expectations have they created about the position? Or on the other hand, how frustrated have they left their customers (either internal or externals)? Were they long-term thinkers or short-term thinkers? Have they built good foundations for the position or would you be starting all over.
This is also valid for the company. Is it a company that has invested in the long term or not? Do they have good foundations? Is it a stable company? Does the corporate culture favour stability and steadiness or high flexibility and constant changes? No answer to the last question is really good or bad but you need to determine if the answer suits you.
It is not always possible to get this part of the job

interview preparation done. In that case, get ready to ask some of these questions during the interview.

5. **Whether the land is fat or lean?**
This part has to do with the profitability of the company. Are they doing well financially? What are the results? Did the previous position holder maximize the potential of the position.

6. **And whether there is any wood?**
In other words, which resources will be available to succeed in the job? What are the goals and vision of the company? Do they seem to have a bright future?

And lastly, Moses instructed the 12 spies to bring some of the fruits from the land. We are not told from the Scriptures if they did but one thing they brought back for sure was a grasshoper complex. Don't ever do that, it may cost you 40 years in your career...:-).

The objective of doing some preliminary research as part of the job interview preparation is not to get intimated by the competition. There may be giants in the land but there is a strategy to overcome giants as well.

Online Reputation Management

One of the most important job interview preparation keys is online reputation management.

We live in the information age and it's quite easy nowadays to find information online about anything and anybody.

People leave a lot of information on the internet and they don't realize that many recruiting companies make online research on candidates before job interview.

What are the social networks such as Facebook, Linkedin, Twitter revealing about you?

To illustrate the power of good reputation management, let's learn from the Bible how an unemployed young woman by the name of Ruth, in a time of severe recession (famine) found favor with a prospective employer because of the reputation that preceded her.

(Rut 2:10 NKJV) So she fell on her face, bowed down to the ground, and said to him, "Why have I found favor in your eyes, that you should take notice of me, since I am a foreigner?"

(Rut 2:11 NKJV) And Boaz answered and said to her, "It has been fully reported to me, all that you have done for your mother-in-law since the death of your husband, and how you have left your father and your mother and the land of your birth, and have come to a people whom you did not know before.

(Rut 2:12 NKJV) The LORD repay your work, and a full reward be given you by the LORD God of Israel, under whose wings you have come for refuge."

This young woman, under severe disadvantages (a widow, foreigner and unemployed on a foreign land) found favor with a prospective employer (Boaz) thanks to the good reputation report made about her.

Which report are the social networks and search engines making about you?

Is it a good or a bad one?

Is it potentially embarrassing?

First, you need to google yourself to find all the facts.

If the online reputation reports are quite positive or at least neutral, good for you. This is already a good start! But there is still a way to improve it.

If the reports are rather bad or potentially damaging to your job search, then you need to take strong steps to change it.

Maybe, you created a group on facebook named "how to steal your employer without been caught"

Or "I am lazy and I love it". You would be surprised which kind of crazy groups are out there on the social networks.

Once that bad report is on the cyberspace, it is very difficult to revert it. You cannot write a request to google to remove it.

So, which effective online reputation management steps could you take during your job interview preparation?

Don't despair, there is a solution.

First of all, remove all the negative information you have posted. Delete these crazy groups if you ever created any. This will at least contribute to contain the damage, and possibly fix your online reputation.

But in most cases, these steps are far from been enough. Even if you delete the groups, Google still knows about them and could display them during a search.

Therefore, you need to take as a second step to publish positive information on you social networks account. Why not display some good achievements from previous or current job?

Did you get any good appraisals or rewards? Let it be known but be careful not to go overboard as well. It needs to be contextual as much as possible and believable.

Finally, in order to get a good online reputation in the mid to long term range, the most excellent way is to create a website to share about your experience or passion in relation to your field.

For example, If you are an analyst, why not create a website on the theme: "successful analysis", "the power of good analysis" or "analysis for dummies".

You can make research to find a niche where you website can achieve decent and even good ranking on the search engines.

Using a thematic website about your profession as a job interview preparation step will build your credibility online like nothing else.

And don't forget to mention the URL of your website on your resume.

Another side benefit of the thematic website step is the ability to earn some additional revenues on the side.

Job Interview Help - From prisoner to prime minister!

How can you be appointed from prisoner to price-minister in few minutes, let's get some job interview help by looking at the career of a young man named Joseph, whose story is related in the book of Genesis. Some extrapolation has been made from the original text, but everything is based from true events in the life of Joseph, as related in the Scriptures.

Once upon a time, there was a very prosperous corporation, Egypt Inc. There came a time of big troubles for this company and the CEO set out to find the management consultant who could help solve the problem.

But the situation only got from bad to worse as none of the numerous top flying consultants hired managed to understand the root cause of the problems.

Pharaoh, the CEO, was devastated as the future of the company seemed in jeopardy and he could not see the light out of the tunnel.

But just when everything looked desperate, he got referred to a young immigrant. At this point, Pharaoh was desperate enough to try anything. Very skeptical as you can imagine, he did not expect much from the job interview.

Alone in his office, while waiting for the young man, Pharaoh's thoughts were on the good old days when profits were high and he was highly and unanimely appraised for his outstanding leadership skills.

He made it often to the 'entrepreneur of the year' club. And now, here he was, with the future of the great company he built in the hands of a young immigrant!

As he shook his head in disbelief and started to laugh at the absurdity of the situation, there was a knock at the door. One of his assistant came in, introducing the young man for the job interview.

Wow! Pharaoh's first impression was not good. Even though, he was freshly shaved and properly dressed, the young man didn't look like the experts and consultants he was accustomed to hire.He was certainly not going to provide any job interview help to this young immigrant but he had nothing to loose after all.

Pharaoh proceeded to shake his hand and invited him to take the seat in front of him.
- Young man, he asked, what is your name ?
- Joseph, he answered calmly
- Where are you from ?
- I am from a far away country
- Ok, tell me about your past experiences ? where were you before ? what brought you here ?
- Before appearing before you, I was in prison, sir! Pharaoh could not believe it.
- You said what ?
- I was in prison, sir! repeated with a strange assurance (under the circumstances) Joseph
- In prison ? you must be a man of low morality. what took you there ?
- Sir, I could tell you I was unjustly put to prison, under the false accusation of rape. But you will certainly not believe a word I said.

But would it matter if I can help solve the big issues Egypt Inc is facing currently ?
- Young man, what makes you think you can succeed

where all the experts and gurus failed to even identify the root cause of our current difficulties, less design a proper solution?

- Sir, when I was in prison, I solved a similar issue for two of your managers

- Hum, Hum, Pharaoh nodded perplexly, and where did you work before the prison ?

- I was an employer in Potiphar Inc. I was assets manager there

- what was your experience before joining Potiphar Inc ?

- Sir, Potiphar Inc was actually my first job experience.

Before that, I was still in my parent's house. But even there, I was faced twice myself with the similar problem you are currently experiencing. All I could at the time was to share them with my family

- Again, young man, you seem to know already what is the root cause what makes you think you are the best candidate for the job?

- Sir, actually, I cannot solve the problem. But I do know somebody I am connected to, that can. He knows everything and with his help, you problem will be solved

- Great, all right, that's a big statement, you'll have to prove it before the job interview ends. But before, I want to know more about you. What are your weaknesses?

- I have a lot of them but none is relevant to the job

- What are your strenghts, then ?

- Only one of my strenghts is relevant to the job. I have complete trust in my friend, the one I mentioned earlier, and his capacities. He has never failed me and will never do.

Wherever I went, He was with me. when I was thrown in a pit, He was there. When I was sold as a slave, He was there. He got me promoted from slave to assets manager at Potiphar Inc, my first job, without any job interview.

When I was unjustly accused and thrown into prison, He was still there to cheer me up. He got me promoted as manager in the prison.
This is how I got to solve your manager's problems in prison. Now Sir, give me the job and with the help of my friend,your problems will be solved. There are no problems too big for Him to handle. If you give me the job, you get two persons for the price of one.
- Ok, Joseph, you get the job. Now, let me describe the problem to you in details...

What an amazing story!. In a minute, we will look at what kind of job interview help we can get from it. Off course, you know the end of the story, how Joseph got the job, did outstanding well and was promoted as vice-president of Egypt Inc. The rest is history.

From this story, you can pick up few points on key job interview questions you will face and how to answer them.

Let's inventory them to get some job interview help:
- Tell me about your past experiences, where were you before ?
- What brought you here ?
- What are your strenghts ?
- What are your weaknesses ?
- Tell me what qualify you for the job, why are you the best candidate for the job

Joseph's answers to the job interview questions were :
- open and honest. He did not hide the prison episode
- focused and relevant to the position
- He turned around the biggest objections (you must be a man of low morality) by answering them briefly and then putting the focus back to the position
- He even answered a question before it was asked:
Even before getting his first job at Potiphar Inc, he was faced with similar issue facing Egypt Inc (dream interpretation). That makes up for his lack of formal

education in dream interpretation. No doubt, young Joseph got great job interview help from His friend. That's how he could secure a job of vice-president of Egypt Inc while been interviewed as a prisoner!

There is a lot of hidden wisdom in the Word of God that can be used as job interview help to suceed in the marketplace. Stay with us on this amazing discovery. Wisdom is really the principal thing!

Job Interview Steps

Let's discover from Luke 5:1-8 typical job interview steps by looking at the calling of the first disciples.

The Calling of the First Disciples

1One day as Jesus was standing by the Lake of Gennesaret,[a]with the people crowding around him and listening to the word of God, 2he saw at the water's edge two boats, left there by the fishermen, who were washing their nets. 3He got into one of the boats, the one belonging to Simon, and asked him to put out a little from shore. Then he sat down and taught the people from the boat. 4When he had finished speaking, he said to Simon, "Put out into deep water, and let down[b] the nets for a catch."

5Simon answered, "Master, we've worked hard all night and haven't caught anything. But because you say so, I will let down the nets."

6When they had done so, they caught such a large number of fish that their nets began to break. 7So they signaled their partners in the other boat to come and help them, and they came and filled both boats so full that they began to sink.

8When Simon Peter saw this, he fell at Jesus' knees and said, "Go away from me, Lord; I am a sinful man!" 9For he and all his companions were astonished at the catch of fish they had taken, 10and so were James and John, the sons of Zebedee, Simon's partners.

Then Jesus said to Simon, "Don't be afraid; from now on you will catch men." 11So they pulled their boats up on shore, left everything and followed him.

As we can see in the beginning of the verse, Jesus just started his company and was at work, teaching the

Word of God. He was certainly led by the Spirit to the lake of Gennesaret. There, he noticed two potential new employees for his startup: Simon and his brother Andrew. He proceeded to interview them, without them even been aware of what was hapenning.

The first step of the interview was to show Simon and Andrew what the company was all about.
Been alone in the boat with Jesus, Simon experienced first hand the product of the company: the Word of God. There are some companies using this job interview technique today. This is common in the sales area for example where the prospective sales representative spends one day or few hours on the road with the hiring manager, watching him selling and dealing with customers and prospects. At the end of this step, the candidate should know enough about the job and the company to determine if he wanted to pursue any further. This first job interview step sets also the stage for the rest of the process and the job interview questions to ask.

In the second job interview step, Jesus tested Simon on the most important skills needed for the job:
- Ability to learn from mistakes
- Willingness to think outside the box and receive new ideas
- Been teachable
- Willingness to follow instructions even when not understood or agreed upon

Simon passed the test sucessfully, even though he did it reluctantly. This phase is one of the key job interview steps. It can be used as job interview screening technique that will determine if you get invited to a second interview or not.
Now begun the third job interview step. Jesus showed Peter the impact of his company and product on its customer's life.

He showed him that **"man doesn't live on bread alone but from every word that comes from the mouth of God".** In the first phase, Simon learned how Jesus delivered his products and services. He also learned about the features of the product, what the Word of God says.

In this third step however, he learned the impact on individuals. He learned that when you obey the Word of God, when you apply it to your life, things begin to change. The impossible becomes possible. They had tried all night to catch fish without any success. These were trained, professional fishermen. By obeying the Word of God, they got so many fishes that their boat begun to sink.

In this third step, Simon is tested on some additional, more advanced skills:
- How to handle the unexpected (he didn't expect the boat to be so full, possibly that never happened to him before but he quickly found a creative solution).
- Team work and cooperation skills (Simon realized he could not do it alone and sought help from the team).
- Humility on the job & good knowledge of his weaknesses ("go away from me, Lord, I am a sinful man"). He passed this final test successfully and got hired for the position "fisherman of men".

what an amazing job interview. It has a lot of teaching on job interview techniques for both candidates and interviewers.

We can also distinguish different job interview steps:
- Learn about the job, the products and services
- Test and/or questions to show first level skills
- More in-depth information on the job and the company (learn about the impact of the company's products and services)
- Test and/or questions on more advanced skills

Answer to job interview question on stress

One of the toughest job interview question is related to how you cope with stressful situations on the job.
The question can be also presented in other ways such as: "Describe a situation when you were faced with high stress and how you handled it"
As usual, let's get some wisdom from the Book.

Luke 22 39Jesus went out as usual to the Mount of Olives, and his disciples followed him. 40On reaching the place, he said to them, "Pray that you will not fall into temptation." 41He withdrew about a stone's throw beyond them, knelt down and prayed, 42"Father, if you are willing, take this cup from me; yet not my will, but yours be done." 43An angel from heaven appeared to him and strengthened him. 44And being in anguish, he prayed more earnestly, and his sweat was like drops of blood falling to the ground

Hebrews12 2Let us fix our eyes on Jesus, the author and perfecter of our faith, who for the joy set before him endured the cross, scorning its shame, and sat down at the right hand of the throne of God.

I tend to think that what happened in the Mount of Olives was the most stressful situation of Jesus' life. It was really a pivotal moment. The Scripture says 'his sweat was like drops of blood falling to the ground'. I don't know about you, but how more stressful can it get than that? It's the only record in the Scriptures of Jesus sweating blood. So, it was a time of intense stress and pressure.

This stress was due to the fact that He saw what was coming at Him, the rejection, the persecution, the separation from the Father and the horrible death on the cross. He was faced with a very painful decision: to willingly submit to the will of the Father (his employer in corporate context) with the full knowledge of what that implies in terms of pain and suffering.

So he says "Father, if you are willing, take this cup from me…" BUT in the same verse, there is a semi comma and then the dramatic focus shift "; yet not my will, but yours be done.". Hebrews12:2 tells us what caused the shift to occur. It was "the joy set before Him". He set his eyes on the vision and the impact it was going to have on people. He visualized past the crucifixion, He visualized resurrection day, ascension day, and the return to the Father. He visualized millions of people getting saved and having hope again. He visualized the joy in heaven among the angels. He visualized the rewards and weighted them against the pain.

Then He got peace in His mind. The matter got instantly settled. I believe victory over the cross was already made at that moment because it all starts in the mind. The mind is the battlefield.

Three important elements in your answer to the job interview question on handling stressful and difficult situations at work:

- First of all, stay connected to your management. Jesus went to a solitary place to have undisturbed meeting with the CEO. **Your answer should demonstrate your commitment to ensure you are still in alignment with the company vision.**

- Secondly, get the help of your support team but understand that ultimately you must take responsibility. **Your answer to the job interview question should also demonstrate your team work and cooperation skills.**

- Thirdly, after the two points above are covered, your success came by putting your eyes on the vision (and its impact) and determined that it was worthwhile.

Don't hesitate to be more specific in your answer. This is a great way to turn a tough job interview question to your advantage by showing your understanding of the importance of the company vision, team work and determination to press on in difficult times.

Most common of the top job interview questions - Where are you?

During your job search, one of the top job interview questions you cannot escape can be found in the Bible, in the book of Genesis, after the fall of man. Let's remind the related verses:

Genesis 3:8-13
8 Then the man and his wife heard the sound of the LORD God as he was walking in the garden in the cool of the day, and they hid from the LORD God among the trees of the garden. 9 But the LORD God called to the man, **"Where are you?"**

10 He answered, "I heard you in the garden, and I was afraid because I was naked; so I hid."

11 And he said, "Who told you that you were naked? Have you eaten from the tree that I commanded you not to eat from?"

12 The man said, "The woman you put here with me— she gave me some fruit from the tree, and I ate it."

13 Then the LORD God said to the woman, "What is this you have done?" The woman said, "The serpent deceived me, and I ate."

This fundamental question: **WHERE ARE YOU?** may come through one form or another but it cannot be avoided during any serious job interview. A job interview is an encounter between two destinies: yours and the prospective employer, trying to determine if their future is somehow related.
So, inevitably, one of the top job interview questions

from both sides should be: **WHERE ARE YOU?** Let's examine this top job interview question from both perspectives.

Question from the employer to the candidate: Where are you?

The employer wants to know: ' Mr future employee of mine, where are you in your career? what are your greatest motivational needs at this point? Why did you leave your previous job? What are you exactly after in your new job search ? Which skills have you developed so far from your past experiences?'

This is a series of questions to be answered honestly, openly and obviously a good preparation would help you do just that. If we go back to the Bible verses quoted previously, Adam had been given a job by God to dominate the earth, to subdue it and keep it. But he was found out of position. Instead of been in a position of authority, he was hiding.

So God had to ask him the big question: **WHERE ARE YOU?** The purpose was for him to give an account of his past experiences. He admitted he failed to carry out successfully his responsabilities. But of course, 'it was not his fault!'. He was naked, he was not equipped, he felt, to do the job properly. Many things to learn from these powerful verses on how not to answer one of this top job interview questions: - Don't ever put the blame on something or somebody else for your own shortcomings
- Even worse, don't blame or criticize your past employer or past colleagues.

Adam blamed his past failures on :
- lack of resources (I was naked)
- past employer (YOU gave me)
- past colleagues (the woman)

Your interviewer will quicky identify himself (herself) with your past employer. Not very good news for you. As we can see later, Eve also found somebody else to blame.

What your interviewer is also looking after by asking this common job interview question (**WHERE ARE YOU?**) is also to see how you use your past experiences (both successes and failures) to your advantage. What did you learn from them ? But it all starts by taking full responsability for them and not blaming somebody else. As long as you stick to this unproper covering (with fig leaves), you will have hard time to provide a proper answer to the most common of the top job interview questions: **WHERE ARE YOU?**

Top job interview question to ask : Where are you?

As a candidate been interviewed, it is also your responsability to ask the employer: **WHERE ARE YOU?**
This top job interview question relates both to the company overall and the position. In your case, if you have done your homework properly, you already know part of the answer. Now, you have the opportunity during the interview to go deeper and demonstrate the level of interest you have in the company.
Where is the company now? (early expansion phase or stabilization phase?)
Where is the position? You need a good answer to those crucial job interview questions. Does the company have good reputation or is it 'hiding'?
Are you comfortable working for this kind of company? you see, in Genesis, God himself covered Adam and Eve. He covered their reputation with the proper covering, something they could not achieve on their own, using fig leaves. Will you be ready to cover your company with a proper covering?

Top job interview questions for managers

Let's have a look at some fascinating answers from the book of Genesis on top Job Interview questions for managers.

Genesis 1: 1 -3
The Beginning 1 In the beginning God created the heavens and the earth. 2 Now the earth was [a] formless and empty, darkness was over the surface of the deep, and the Spirit of God was hovering over the waters.

3 And God said, "Let there be light," and there was light. 4 God saw that the light was good, and He separated the light from the darkness. 5 God called the light "day," and the darkness he called "night." And there was evening, and there was morning—the first day.

One of the top questions you may face during your job interview for a manageurial position is the following : **"Tell me what is the most important quality of a leader"** The book of Genesis answers this question. The first thing God created after the heavens and the earth was the light.**Light speaks of vision**. The Scripture says that God is Light and in Him there is no darkness. God already had the light inside of him since He is Light.
But that light needed to be reflected upon the universe.

A leader must not only have the vision but he must communicate this vision to the people. This is very important. It is so important that we can see clearly the impact of its absence on the company.

The verse says that the earth was formless and empty, darkness was over the surface of the deep.
Without a shared vision, there is confusion.
Without a shared vision, there is not much profit. The company cannot succeed.
When a company is in chaos, the first thing it needs is a management with a clear vision that is communicated and shared with the employees.

In the same way, you have to demonstrate to the hiring manager you have a vision for where you are headed and communicate clearly this vision during the job interview. One job interview question you may also face is : **"where do you see yourself in 5 years or 10 years from now?"** Without the light, without the vision, you cannot provide a clear and coherent answer. Instead, your answer will be "formless and empty".

Make sure all this is clear before you show up for the job interview. This is also true for the hiring manager. He/she should communicate clearly the vision of the company and which part the position plays in fulfilling that vision. When the vision is clear, you can separate the light from the darkness. You know which ones of the interviewees fit the vision best.

The candidate also knows which company/job fits best his own vision for the future, his own career aspiration. This is a win/win. So, get the vision for a successful job interview.
Get the vision to be able to answer properly to one of the top job interview questions.

Job Interview Question - Why You?

To illustrate an important job interview question and how to answer it successfully, let's go again in the Scriptures.

Luke 7:18John's disciples told him about all these things. Calling two of them, 19he sent them to the Lord to ask, "Are you the one who was to come, or should we expect someone else?" 20When the men came to Jesus, they said, "John the Baptist sent us to you to ask, 'Are you the one who was to come, or should we expect someone else?' "

21At that very time Jesus cured many who had diseases, sicknesses and evil spirits, and gave sight to many who were blind. 22So he replied to the messengers, "Go back and report to John what you have seen and heard: The blind receive sight, the lame walk, those who have leprosy[b] are cured, the deaf hear, the dead are raised, and the good news is preached to the poor. 23Blessed is the man who does not fall away on account of me."

How well you answer the type of questions illustrated above can differentiate you from other good candidates with the required qualifications.

The interview went very well so far. You gave a good first impression and managed to establish a good rapport with the interviewer.

Your qualifications and past work experiences seem to be well suited for the position.

And now you start to feel very good about the future outcome.

Moreover, you like the company and the future perspectives of the position.

Beware! It isn't over yet!

Don't ruin all your hard work and preparation by failing to provide a clear, concise and confident answer to the following question: "Why should we hire you instead of the other candidates?"

In marketing term, we would say "What is your unique selling proposition?"

What are the distinct characteristics about you to convince me you are the one I am looking for? "Are you the rare jewel or should I choose somebody else?"

Look at Jesus's answer:

"Go back and report to John what you have seen and heard: The blind receive sight, the lame walk, those who have leprosy[b] are cured, the deaf hear, the dead are raised, and the good news is preached to the poor. 23Blessed is the man who does not fall away on account of me."

John the Baptist was the one who recognized earlier Jesus as the Messiah (the one who was to come) because of a revelation he received from God.

He saw the Holy Spirit coming upon Jesus as a dove.

The Scripture "The Spirit of the Lord is on me, because he has anointed me to preach good news to the poor. He has sent me to proclaim freedom for the prisoners and recovery of sight for the blind, to release the oppressed, to proclaim the year of the Lord's favor"

was fulfilled.

Jesus did not get angry at John, he was not surprised, he did not hesitate in His answer.

He didn't tell him "Remember the testimony you gave earlier about me"

He simply explained that He was doing exactly what the one who was to come should be doing and having great results.

The results were speaking for Him, the results were testifying for Him.

Before starting His ministry, the only testimony He had was that of John received from the Father.

Now, in addition, the facts were also speaking for Him, so that John's doubts are now insignificants.

In the same way, you need to prepare a summary statement explaining why you are the one, why the interviewer should select you among all candidates.

You need to make the statement with confidence, conviction and clarity. It should be based on facts.

In summary:

- Don't get caught off guard by the question "Why should we select you instead of somebody else" but be prepared to answer it

- Don't express any negative emotions in your answer

- Your answer should be precise, concise and facts based

- You should state it with confidence

If you do all the above, and the interview went well to that point, you may just have secured the position.

If you don't get asked the question, you can take the opportunity at the end of the interview to state the same answer if the interviewer asks you if you have any questions.

He should be pleasantly surprised.

Job interview question - dealing with resistance to change

How can you answer effectively to a job interview question on how to deal with resistance to change? Let's pick some precious elements from our reference: the Scriptures

Luke 7:18John's disciples told him about all these things. Calling two of them, 19he sent them to the Lord to ask, "Are you the one who was to come, or should we expect someone else?"

We all like to think that we can easily adapt to changes when they occur. We all think we like change. But the truth is we all have some degree of resistance to change. The RC (Resistance to Change) factor is not a myth. It can be a big problem in the corporate world if not managed properly and dealt with appropriately. So, you should not be surprised to face a job interview question on change and how to manage it.

If you are responsible for a project, you will need to identify the key people whose work will be impacted and make a preliminary assessment of their RC factor and how to get acceptance for the results of your project.

We can see in the verse above John Baptist's perplexity about the changes introduced by Jesus.

It seemed like Jesus was doing everything opposite to what Jesus was used to.
John used to stay in the wilderness and wait for people to come to him.
Jesus was traveling from town to town preaching the good news of the kingdom.
John's disciples used to fast often while Jesus' disciples

never fasted. Jesus got even questioned about this perceived discrepancy.

But like Jesus stated in the book of Matthew 9:17 "Neither do people put new wine into old wineskins. If they do, the skins will burst, the wine will run out and the wineskins will be ruined. No, they pour new wine into new wineskins, and both are preserved"

We should put new wine only into a new wineskin. This means you need to prepare the people (the wineskins) to be ready for the new wine that you want to give them.
Otherwise, the wine will burst through the wineskin and get lost.
In other words, the results of all the team's hard work will be ruined if you simply ignore the RC factor.
It is ironic that John Baptist was preaching a message of repentance (changing of thought patterns) but didn't realize the full extend of the changes that were coming.
John was asking people to change from old wineskins into new wineskins, but was himself caught by surprise by the taste (aspects) of the new wine.

It was a major shift, so dramatic that Jesus would go as far as to say that the least person in the kingdom (the cheapest new wineskin) was greater than John Baptist (the most expensive old wineskin).

From the Scriptures, we see a character, Andrew, who made the shift quickly. He was first John's disciple but upon hearing John's testimony, he turned around and followed Jesus, bringing his brother Simon Peter with him.

So, to summarize, if you are the one introducing change, you need to manage it by helping people change from old wineskins into new wineskins. You can do this by demonstrating why change was necessary.

You should give them a good reason to accept your changes.

Jesus' statement about "the least person in the kingdom been greater than John Baptist" gives us a great example of how to do this.

He simply made a dramatic comparison between the old and new and why the new was much better.

He also added "the violent take it by force". In other words, the new wine is so great that people are lining up to get it, they want to be the first ones to have it. In other words, "do you know that many people are trying to convince me to give them this new product first?" "do you know that other departments want to be the first to pilot this new system?"**"Everybody wants this new stuff and they are going out of their way to get it"** "Do you know that people are lining up all night in a queue so they have a chance to get this new device?" **You create a buzz about the product of the change and you will never suffer again from the RC factor.**

Off course, the buzz has to be based on truth, otherwise it will come back to hit you like a boomerang.

Wherever Jesus went, He expressed the culture of the kingdom of God with words but also signs and wonders. Both are necessary if you want to inspire change in people, if you want to overcome the RC factor. If people didn't believe His words, they could see by themselves that what He was offering was far greater.

Another element is to show people that the change you are promoting is actually necessary to get what they want. Nicodemus was already convinced that the new wine was far greater than the old wine. He wanted to have it too. But Jesus shared the main condition: if you want the new, you must be born again: you must accept the change, the radical change.

Let's now try to summarize how we can apply the above in answering effectively the job interview question: how do you deal with resistance to change in the workplace?

The first element in your answer is to **recognize that the RC factor can be a big problem in corporations.** The interviewer should see that you take it seriously. You cannot give a casual answer, in the like "we'll just impose the change on people". Jesus said the RC factor can ruin all of your efforts. The people affected by your project may express their resistance to you openly or not but in all cases, you need to assess it beforehand and anticipate it.

The second element in your answer is to **show how you inspire people to adopt the change by telling them and showing them how the new is superior to the old.** You need to know the people's needs and wants and make demonstration to them on how they will benefit from your project.

The third element in your answer to this job interview question is **the usage of the buzz strategy, when applicable.** People that may display a high RC factor to your project should know that other people are eager to adopt the new. You should conclude your answer to this job interview question by stating that **sometimes, the only way to deal with the RC factor is to impose the change on people.** Nevertheless, it should not be the primary option in most cases.

Since we are leaving on times of great uncertainty, you could face often this job interview question on dealing with resistance to change.

You should then be prepared to answer it effectively and if possible give specific examples from your past experiences when you applied these principles.

Job Interview question - Do you like to work in teams and why ?

The following job interview question is quite common: **Do you like to work in team and why?**

How can we articulate a good answer to this question? Let's examine the Scriptures once again.

Genesis 2:18 The LORD God said, "It is not good for the man to be alone. I will make a helper suitable for him."

God has just completed the creation of his company Earth incorporated and he appointed a project manager by the name of Adam, with the assignment to manage it and rule over it.
Then, in His wisdom, He said that it was not good for man to be alone. He wanted a project team for His project manager. **So, we can say that God puts a high value on team work. Teams are valuable.**

Next, in your answer to this job interview question, you need to argument why teams are valuable. The Scriptures say that one will chase a thousand but two will chase ten thousands. This clearly shows us that the value of an effective team is greater than the sum of values of the individual members.
Effective teamwork yields exponential results and not arithmetic ones. Two will not chase two thousands but...ten thousands because additional value is created by the effective interaction between team members. **In short, teams are valuable because they increase overall productivity.**

The second element we can pick up from the Bible verses above is that**the goal of team work is helping each other**. God said, since it is not good for

man to be alone, I will make him a helper, someone that can help him with the assignment (project) I just gave him to have dominion on the earth.
He didn't say I will make for him an opponent, someone to criticize him or a competitor.
This tells us that for a team to be effective in yielding exponential results the members must be helpful to each other, they must support each other.

The third element from the verse, useful for answering the teamwork job interview question, is that the helper must be suitable for him.
Yes, it is not good for man to be alone but this doesn't mean that I can just team him up with anybody.
Otherwise, God could have instructed Adam to team up with the animals.
To be effective, teams must be made of the right mix of people. Team members must be suitable to each other.
Look at this amazing statement by Adam "This is bone of my bones and flesh of my flesh and she shall be called woman…" Adam didn't say that about any of the animals that God presented to him in order that he name them.
The "bone of my bones and flesh of my flesh" means "we belong together", it denotes a high team spirit. It means if you are hurt, I am hurt, if you are fine, I am fine because we are one.

We now have a perfect team with a strong sense of belonging. This team can operate at very high level if it keeps this team spirit.

In summary, our answer to this job interview question can be structured as follows:
- Teams are valuable because they can yield exponential results
- But in order to achieve this increased productivity and effectiveness, they must be of the right mix and good team spirit must be maintained at all costs

Job Interview Question - 3 wishes

One tricky job interview question you could be asked is the following: "If I could grant you 3 wishes, what would they be?"

This is a very tricky interview question. It will not be good enough to avoid egocentric answers such as "give me the job, a good salary, benefits". Your answer should be better than that.

Now, let's look in the Scriptures how the wise man Solomon came up with a brilliant answer to a similar job interview question.

1 Kings 3:5-13: One night in Gibeon the Lord appeared to Solomon in a dream. God said " Ask for whatever you want me to give you".

Solomon answered "You have shown great kindness to your servant, my father David, because he was faithful to you and righteous and upright in heart. You have continued this great kindness to him and have given him a son to sit on his throne this very day.

Now, lord my God, you have made your servant king in place of my father David. But I am only a little child and do not know how to carry out my duties.

So give your servant a discerning heart to govern your people and to distinguish between right and wrong. For who is able to govern this great people of yours?"

First of all, Solomon expressed his gratitude to the interviewer for giving him the opportunity. We could say that he found something good to praise the interviewer about. In your case, it could even be something positive you found about the company during your preparative research work. But in any case start with a praise or gratitude.

Then Solomon plainly mentioned his weaknesses in regards to the job position (young age and lack of experience). He explained the challenges of the position (difficulty to lead a large group of employees in his case).

Then he asks for what was required to overcome these challenges despite his weaknesses.

This is simply brilliant:

- He showed a thorough understanding of the job and its challenges

- He showed honesty by talking openly about his weaknesses

- He showed, moreover, a great committment and motivation to succeed in the job

The next verse said that God was pleased about the answer and the fact that it was focused on the success of the job and not centered on the interviewee.

So, in conclusion, if you face a similar job interview question, use your answer as an opportunity to demonstrate that you know yourself very well, that you also understand the challenges of the job been advertised and what it takes to succeed in it.

This is even more important if you have already perceived some objections/doubts in the mind of your interviewer. This could be lack of experience, like Solomon, or any other disadvantages in your candidature.

Don't however go to the extreme and start to mention all your weaknesses. simply pick one that was already mentioned by the hiring manager (either implicitely or explicitely) and show him it will not prevent you to succeed in the job because you have an action plan.

I hope you begin to see that every job interview question you face should be used as an opportunity to demonstrate why you are the best candidate for the job.

If you do this consistently, you are well on your way to get hired.

And off course, you can only do that successfully to the extend that you came to the interview well prepared.

Job Interview Question - Giving Feedback

If you are looking to get a job as a manager, you may not escape a job interview question in the like of:"How do you give negative feedback to subordinates?" OR"As a manager, how do you handle bad performance by your team members"

In the book of Genesis, we can learn how God handles a similar case.

Gen 4:3-7In the course of time Cain brought some of the fruits of the soil as an offering to the lord.
4 And Abel also brought an offering—fat portions from some of the firstborn of his flock. The lord looked with favor on Abel and his offering,
5 but on Cain and his offering he did not look with favor. So Cain was very angry, and his face was downcast.

6 Then the lord said to Cain, "Why are you angry? Why is your face downcast?

7 If you do what is right, will you not be accepted? But if you do not do what is right, sin is crouching at your door; it desires to have you, but you must rule over it."

As we see, the company Universe INC. was starting to grow and 2 new employees were hired: Cain first, then Abel second.They were in different departments and came the time to give an account for their results.

The verses above tell us that Abel was commended for his great results while Cain got a bad performance rating.

Cain, the underachiever got very dissastified and sad about his bad rating. Furthermore, he got jealous of Abel, the great employee.

But if we analyze carefully the verse, we can see important principles on how God, the CEO handled this performance appraisal exercise.

If He were to answer a job interview question about giving negative feedback, He would mention the following 3 golden rules:

- First of all, we see that **the feedback has to be timely.** When you perceive bad performance or behavior, do your best to provide feedback while the situation is fresh. That will give the employee the opportunity to make adjustments and improve if he is wise, before the final periodic appraisal. It is wrong, as a manager to wait until the periodic year-end appraisal exercise.

- Second, you need to **make sure to separate the person from the performance or behavior**. It was clearly stated in the verse that the disapproval was on the performance (offering) and not targeted at the employee itself (Cain).

- Third, even if you comply by the second rule, you still need to **be attentive and check how well the feedback was received**. That is how the CEO noticed that the employee got very angry and sad. He took it personally. In most cases, people don't like to receive negative feedback because of low self-esteem and perceive it as an attack on their person. When you notice that the feedback was not well received, you have to provide encouragement and reassurance to the person.

The CEO basically told the "bad" employee Cain: "Look, it's not personal. If you perform well, you will also get a good rating. So, use this as an opportunity to strive".

You can also warn the employee that he is on the way to destroy his career if he persists on the negative attitude.

In conclusion, your answer to the job interview question about giving negative feedback needs to demonstrate the 3 underlying issues mentioned above:

BE TIMELY IN YOUR FEEDBACK

SEPARATE THE PERSON FROM THE BEHAVIOR

MONITOR AND MANAGE POSSIBLE CONSEQUENCES

Job Interview Question - Problem Solving

A job interview question you may face during your job search is the following or something similar: If I select for this position, tell me which steps you would take from your first day at work.

A similar question could be: describe a situation where you demonstrated your problem solving skills? How did you do it? Let`s again get to the Book of books to be inspired on how to answer such question in an efficient manner.

Genesis 1 In the beginning God created the heaven and the earth.2 And the earth was without form, and void; and darkness was upon the face of the deep. And the Spirit of God moved upon the face of the waters.3 And God said, Let there be light: and there was light.

The verses above are very inspiring as we see God starting His work in regards to the earth.

Let's see how He proceeded and the steps He took.

- First of all, He made a complete inspection of the business (or department) to see how it was going. (It said the Spirit of God moves upon the face of the waters)

- Then, He identified the problem (the earth was without form and void and darkness was upon the face of the deep). The situation analysis He performed showed a two dimensional problem (darkness & the lack of form which can also be described as chaos). This was not at all according to His standards.

- After discovering the two dimensional problem (darkness and chaos), He started to make changes step by step in a very orderly fashion. He prioritized the tasks He wanted to take and then started to implement the changes. He decided to address the darkness problem first by creating light. Then He went on to address the chaos problem step by step.

- One very important fact to take out from the text is that He chose to handle the darkness problem on his own. But for the chaos problem, He chose to delegate to man after creating a prototype for him so he duplicate it.

- Another key takeaway (if you would read the subsequent verses) is that after completing each task, He stepped back and evaluated the results to validate it against His own standards of excellence. So He used appraisal words such as (It was good) or (It was very good).

If you had done your preparation correctly for the job interview, you should know which problems the position is supposed to solve.The problem solving job interview question should not take you by surprise at all. The need which created the position could be getting new customers, retain existing customers, replacing an employee who was not performing well or who was promoted, etc.

You should know which problems your position is supposed to solve. If not, you should ask the hiring manager during the interview to tell you.
Once you know what are the problems, you can ask more details about it, or alternatively you will offer, once hired, to investigate and determine all the dimensions related to the issues.

The biggest takeway from the reference text is the long term thinking demonstrated. In your

answer to problem solving job interview question, show that you are not only interested in implementing a solution. Demonstrate also you will think of taking extra steps to prevent the issue from reoccuring.

The creation of man was the step taken to have somebody responsible for keeping order and avoid the chaos problem to reocurr.

Note also it was the only highest appraisal (Very good) whereas the solution itself is only rate das good.

Let`s repeat to make it clear because it is so critical.
In your answer to the interviewer, demonstrate your long-term thinking and proactive skills by having a final task with the objective to systematize the resolution of the problem.
In other words, mention that you will investigate and put in place mechanisms to ensure the issue will not reoccur.

If you are being interviewed for a salesman position for example, you can mention that you will plan and start a marketing campaign but you shouldn't stop there. Demonstrate your excellency by suggesting to put in place a system to get continuous flow of new customers.

This will definitively put you one head above the crowd of other candidates and increase your chances to get hired for the position. The interviewer will really appreciate your forward thinking.

Before closing, you should remember that your overall goal is to use every job interview question as an opportunity to differentiate yourself. If you consistently do that throughout the job interview, the success of your job search is right across the corner.

Job Interview Question to ask - How do you do it here?

There is an important job interview question you should ask the interviewer. Let's discover from the Scriptures by analyzing the interaction between Moses and God.

Exodus 33:13 NIV
If you are pleased with me, teach me your ways so I may know you and continue to find favor with you. Remember that this nation is your people."

Moses is asking God to teach him His ways so he may know and please Him. In corporate terms, the job interview question can be something like this:

What is your corporate culture?

What are the values of the company ?

Which style of management is valued ?

Do you value more autonomy or ability to stick to directive instructions ?

What are the key success criterias for this position ?

Remember that the key goal of the job interview is to find out if you have the right qualifications and also if there is a match between the corporate culture and your own values.

Usually, your preliminary research before the interview should give you information about the corporate culture of the hiring company. Most companies communicate plainly to the outside world about their values. It could be innovation, social responsibility, focus on customer satisfaction, focus on quality, excellence or any other. You can find from the corporate website.

But there are still many things you cannot find out from the outside. There are still some elements of the company values or corporate culture that are only known to the employees. If you would ask any employee, they could tell you: this is how we do it here!

During the interview, you need to find as much as possible through your questions.

You should be wise on how you formulate the question thought. Don't, off course, blantly ask : what is your corporate culture ?You can say : In my preliminary research, I found out that innovation is one of your key values. How does the position fit into that ?

The interviewer will be pleasantly surprised that you took the time to do your homework beforehand.

You will also show him from this job interview question on corporate culture that you understand the end objective of the interview.

Many candidates wrongly assume that the right qualifications are the only criteria. You will differentiate yourself from such group of candidates.

Make sure in your thank you letter that you mention the matching between the corporate culture and values of the company and your own values. You can also remind the hiring manager that you thrived in a job from your past experiences in a company with similar culture.

If your qualifications for the positions are suitable, that one often neglected question may

be your competitive advantage over other equally qualified candidates.

Common Job Interview Question: What are your weaknesses?

A job interview question that is almost guaranteed to be asked is the following :
What are your weaknesses ?

Usually, the interviewer will first ask you about your strengths. Most interviewees can handle the strength question easily.

But when it comes to the weaknesses question, most candidates are embarassed. You don't want to say anything that will ruin all your job searching efforts.

Nevertheless, there is no need to be embarassed by this job interview question. Let's turn to the Scriptures, as usual, to pick up some principles that will help us provide a good answer to this question.

Matthew 16
15 "But what about you?" he asked. "Who do you say I am?"
16 Simon Peter answered, "You are the Messiah, the Son of the living God."
17 Jesus replied, "Blessed are you, Simon son of Jonah, for this was not revealed to you by flesh and blood, but by my Father in heaven.

22 Peter took him aside and began to rebuke him. "Never, Lord!" he said. "This shall never happen to you!"
23 Jesus turned and said to Peter, "Get behind me, Satan! You are a stumbling block to me; you do not have in mind the concerns of God, but merely human concerns."

From the text above, let's analyze how Simon Peter

might answer truthfully this common job interview question about weaknesses. In the first part, he was the only one to answer correctly about the true identity of Jesus. He got praised for it.

He displayed great confidence by answering without any hesitation while the remaining disciples were scratching their heads.

Jesus told him that he got his inspiration directly from the Holy Spirit. I guess Peter felt quite good about that appraisal.

But then, he went a little overboard with it. When the Master was explaining them what must happen later, Peter taught he knew better.

After all, he is inspired, right? He got connection with the highest possible source. He got something way above the other disciples.
So, with the same confidence, he proceeded to rebuke his master.
And the appraisal he got that time was not so good. He must have taught: **Ouch! I blew it!**

Now, here's the principle you should use in your answer to the weaknesses interview question.

- First of all, avoid any answers such as `I don't know` or even worse `I can't think of any right now`. This will show a lack of truthfulness. We all know about our strengths and weaknesses.

- But on the same time, don`t go to the other extreme and start to enumerate every bad thing you know about yourself.

- What you should do is mention a weakness that is a strength gone overboard. When asked about his strengths, Peter may say: confidence, boldness, assertiveness. And then, to the weakness question, he might reply that sometimes he gets too confident and make mistakes and say things he shouldn`t say. He can then continue to say how he corrects the damage afterwards.

You should always mention what you do to mitigate possible bad consequences of the weakness.

So, be prepared and don`t be caught by surprise when asked this common job interview question. Many candidates have stumbled upon it, but it should not be your case after what you have just learned.

I hope this will help you succeed in your job search and get the ideal job for you.

Top Job Interview Questions

Biblical answer to one of the top job interview questions for project managers: "What is the greatest project management skill?"

Genesis 11 The Tower of Babel 1 Now the whole world had one language and a common speech. 2 As men moved eastward, [a] they found a plain in Shinar [b] and settled there. 3 They said to each other, "Come, let's make bricks and bake them thoroughly." They used brick instead of stone, and tar for mortar. 4 Then they said, "Come, let us build ourselves a city, with a tower that reaches to the heavens, so that we may make a name for ourselves and not be scattered over the face of the whole earth."

5 But the LORD came down to see the city and the tower that the men were building. 6 The LORD said, "If as one people speaking the same language they have begun to do this, then nothing they plan to do will be impossible for them. 7 Come, let us go down and confuse their language so they will not understand each other."

8 So the LORD scattered them from there over all the earth, and they stopped building the city. 9 That is why it was called Babel [c] —because there the LORD confused the language of the whole world. From there the LORD scattered them over the face of the whole earth.

From the few verses above, we can say without any doubt that it is**communication skills**, the ability to communicate the vision clearly.

According to Project Management Institute, communication is key to successsful project management and its importance is directly proportional to the size of the team.

If there are N people working on a given project, the number of communication channels is N*(N-1)/2.

This means for example if you have 10 people in the team, you have 45 different communication channels. There are 45 times chances of miscommunication that could negatively impact the project deliverables and timing.

Your project is in jeopardy if there is confusion, if the team members don't understand each other.

This issue goes even beyond speaking the same language because same words don't mean the same thing for different people.

As a project manager, you have to relate to your team, to understand where they are coming from. Their personality profile also plays a big role in interpersonal understanding.

From the same verses, we can see the impact of great communication on the project team. It creates a sense of unity, a great team spirit.

The people on this tower of Babel project are described as "one". This was made possible by them speaking the same language, by them understanding each other perfectly. And we can see afterwards, when their languages got confused, the unity disappeared, there was now poor team spirit and they had to separate themselves.

We can also see from above verses that these people had a project plan, they were already in the project execution phase. This brings one additional element to the surface. The importance of communication skills is even more critical if as a project manager, you join a project you didn't initiate, for example in the execution phase.